Real Estate Investor's Pocket Guide

Tax strategies and Money Making Tips for Rental Property Owners

Carlos Fraser, EA
Cynthia Lubin, CPA

Published in the United States by KH Publishers.

ISBN 978-1-953237-17-0

Printed in the United States of America

www.khpublishers.com

Cover & Interior design by Dez Carter, Designs by Dez

First Paperback Edition, July 2021

Dedication

This book is dedicated to my family and friends who put up with my geeky accounting talk on a regular basis.

—Cynthia

This book is dedicated to my wife, Ntianu Fraser. Without your support, advice, and hard-hitting conversations, my contribution to this book would never have made it out of my head.

To my two son's Kymani & Kooper Fraser, you gave me the strength to stay up at night and get my writing done, to be an even bigger hero in your eyes.

To my mother, father, and little sister, you believed in me when in the days of Holland road.

—Carlos

To the real estate investors reading this book, we hope these money-making tax strategies fill your pockets.

Thank you!

Contents

PREFACE

Thank you for purchasing The Real Estate Investor's Pocket Guide. This book came about from countless interactions with frustrated buy-and-hold real estate investors who did not see the returns they expected after years of owning rental properties. We realized that there were three main issues:

- Not keeping the right records or any records at all. For example, a new client would come into our office, and we would ask them, "What were your expenses for advertising?" The client would look to the left, shrug his or her shoulders, and say, "Maybe about $50 to $70." But in reality, after going over their monthly expenses with them, it turned out that they spent $150 or more. Keeping accurate records and updating them on a monthly basis will prevent you from missing out on any allowable deductions at tax-filing time. We understand keeping monthly records is a pain, but the amount of money you "leave on the table" by not doing this, can be thousands of dollars.

- Not knowing that every (yes, every) expense is deductible. People have the misconception that some expenses are not deductible. But, everything from the ink, paper, staples, printers, and even your computer, is deductible. Furthermore, the mileage it takes to drive to the post office, job sites, or even the hardware store is deductible. You may even deduct a trip to Hawaii to look for a new property is deductible. Lunch at your favorite restaurant with a potential contractor is deductible. Last but not least, this book is, you guessed it, deductible!

- Not having the right accountant on your team. We noticed that no one had taken the time to explain the big picture the way we will in this book. We get it; taxes are not the easiest concept to follow, but for whatever reason, tax accountants love it, and a good one will take the time to research your situation and explain your options clearly.

We understand everyone is in a different phase of his or her real estate investment journey. However, if you fit into one of the following categories, then this book is for you:

- You're a solo real estate investor.

- You want to pay the least amount of taxes.

- You want your tax return to be audit-proof.

- You want to know what is deductible and

what is not.

- You want to learn time and money saving strategies to keep good records.

Even if you don't fit into one of the above categories but have invested in real estate, perhaps for years, you can still gain a lot from this book.

Before we jump in, here is a concept you will need to know early on in your real estate investment journey as it is the underlying theme for every purchase you make and expense you wish to deduct:

REASONABLE, ORDINARY, AND NECESSARY EXPENSES

Do you remember the last time you received a refund for something? What was the first thing you had to prove? You had to prove when you purchased the item so you could get the refund. If you could not produce a receipt, you were either stuck with the item or given a partial refund. Either way, you were at a loss. Tax deductions are no different. In the infamous words of Whitney Houston, "Show me the receipts"!

With your rental property, record keeping is a must. It will make you audit-proof, and you will be able to make more educated decisions with cash flow and investments in the future. Per the tax law, you have the burden of proof that you received income and incurred expenses. You must have evidence such as receipts, canceled checks, or paid bills to support your expenses. You'll need additional evidence for travel, gifts, and auto expenses, which we'll explain in the coming chapters. Here are some quick record keeping hacks:

- Purchase an on-line document storage platform. We recommend apps such as *QuickBooks for Small Business*. Applications such as this provide a simple and convenient way to record your expenses and maintain the evidence.

- Record your income. Income record keeping is very easy. All you need is a copy of the lease and the corresponding monthly payment documents.

  » If you are paid via check, copy the check before you deposit it.

  » If you are paid via cash, get a cash receipt book and provide the tenant with a receipt, and keep a copy for yourself.

  » If you are paid electronically (Zelle, Cash App, etc.), you can use your bank statement as proof as long as the sender information is displayed and the payment is consistent with the lease. If the sender information is not displayed, you should have something that ties it to the tenant.

- Expenses paid by the tenant are included in lieu of income. Keep a copy of the expenses because it will be included in income and expenses. We will talk more about this later.

- If you and the tenant agree to exchange property or services for rent, you will keep a copy of the agreement signed and confirm the fair market value of the service.

Record your expenses! Expenses can be overwhelming, particularly if you don't know what's deductible and what's not. Our advice is to **record everything**. This is vital if you are going to use an accountant to file your tax return. In the coming chapters, we will break down each deductible expense and build it back up so you can have a solid foundation. We know this seems overwhelming. But, this pocket guide will make everything clear so you can be a savvy and money-making real estate professional in no time! So let's get started.

This book is written in a story format. We believe that storytelling helps with learning. Furthermore, a story well-told is remembered more accurately and for far longer than dry flat facts and figures. Storytelling is the oldest form of teaching, dating back to African history. So, we would love for this book to have roots in your brain.

Changes in tax laws and rates may affect some parts of this book; a change in tax law is accounted for in the period of enactment. The retroactive effects cannot be recognized in our book and instead will be reflected in future versions of the book and on our website. In addition, we expect that if tax law changes do happen, the concepts will remain the same. This material has been prepared for informational purposes only. You should consult your own tax, legal, and accounting advisors before engaging in any transaction.

Whether you are a buy-and-hold investor, an investor who fully rents out your property, or a live-in landlord, the concerns are similar. Make more money, maximize deductions, and pay fewer taxes. With that said, let's meet the characters. Michael and Melissa are in different phases of their real estate investment venture. Frustrated with the outcomes of their previous tax returns, they have both decided to work with expert tax and real estate professionals, Cynthia and Carlos. Their goal is to ensure they do not miss out on any deductions and other tax-saving opportunities.

Michael is meeting with Cynthia, and Melissa is meeting with Carlos for the first time. They have compiled prior year returns, receipts, and contracts related to their homes and are ready to dig in. Throughout the book, we will cover some of the most common challenges investors we work with have encountered. While we would love to cover more, this book is intended for use as a pocket guide. We have tried to break down some of the more complex topics with charts, definitions, tips, and other resources.

The best piece of advice we can give as you read this book is that there is no one-size-fits-all solution, so please consult with a tax advisor whom you trust to evaluate your specific situation.

Why This Book
Was Written

Have you been thinking of purchasing an investment property? Do you want to take advantage of all the benefits it offers, such as additional cash flow and tax savings? Or, have you recently purchased a property and did not take advantage of all the deductions you thought you would be able to? Are you somewhere in between and not sure what to do because "your best friend's second aunt, by marriage," told you about all the money she lost in a 'money pit' and scared you off? Well, if anyone has ever experienced any of these scenarios, this book is for you.

Carlos Fraser, EA and partner at Taxko Inc. and Cynthia Lubin, CPA, MBA, Realtor Associate are known as, The Pocket Advisers. They have decided to take all the questions they've received throughout their several years of tax preparation for aspiring investors and compile their knowledge and expertise in this clear and concise pocket guide. *The Pocket Adviser* is a neatly packaged set of answers to some of the most pressing questions from investors (novice to professional) and provide savvy, and money-making strategies investors will be able to easily apply.

Working their way down Schedule E—Supplemental Income and Loss schedule used for real estate and other passive income activities, Carlos and Cynthia aim to help investors decipher this "mysterious" schedule line by line.

Follow the stories of Michael and Melissa, two investors in very different phases of their real estate investor careers. Learn as they work with experts, Cynthia and Carlos, who aim to maximize their deductions and educate them on the ins and outs of real estate tax for investors. The scenarios are easy to understand and give you all the details you need to make the most of your investor experience. This book will be a handy reference for investors who need quick answers, clear guidance, and decision-making references, all while fitting right in your pocket!

CHAPTER 1

MEET THE
REAL ESTATE
PROFESSIONALS

"90% of all millionaires become so through owning real estate"
- Andrew Carnegie

Melissa came into Carlos's office on April 4th of the current year. She just purchased her first investment property. It was a beautiful two-family home in a quiet part of town. She is overwhelmed with all the expenses she has but is unsure what she should deduct or ignore. A friend of hers highly recommended that she speak with Carlos. Melissa will soon find out why.

On March 30th of the current year, Michael walked into Cynthia's office, confused and in need of expert help. He has owned a three-family rental home for two years, lives in one unit, and rents out the other two. His previous accountant never gave him the guidance he needed and instead would always say, "Don't worry about it, I will take care of it," as he rushed Michael out of his office. Michael was referred to Cynthia because of her experience with rental properties and helping real estate professionals maximize their deductions. Cynthia could clearly tell Michael was frustrated about understanding why he had not received the thousands of dollars in refunds everyone said he would get by investing in a rental property. In her years of experience, Cynthia had seen this many times with new clients, and even worse, with clients that previously worked with CPAs who left them confused and frustrated.

While the previous preparers had done everything correctly on the return, they failed to properly educate the client on all of the deductions available to them.

Fortunately for Michael, Cynthia excelled in the accurate preparation of tax returns and effectively educated her clients on what they were doing and what they should expect. After calming Michael down, Cynthia started at the beginning. Going back to the prior year's return, Cynthia walked him through Schedule E: Supplemental Income and Loss - From Rental Real Estate line by line.

TIPS

Hire a professional who understands taxes [for real estate investors] to help you. The easiest way to find a professional is with the free IRS tool called Return Preparer Office (RPO) Directory (https://irs.treasury.gov/rpo/rpo.jsf). This is an excellent tool to find a list of tax professionals in your zip code within at least five miles. Tax pros in the directory have one of the following credentials & qualifications:

- Enrolled agents licensed by the IRS and specialize in tax, preparation, representation, and tax planning.

- Certified Public Accountants licensed by a state board for all accounting ranges, some CPAs specialize in tax preparation, representation, and tax planning.

- Attorneys licensed by a state court and other bodies such as the state bar. Some attorneys specialize in tax, preparations, representation, and tax planning.

Tax professionals use their Preparer Tax Identification Number (PTIN) when they prepare your return or represent you before the IRS. Some tax professionals may not be listed because they do not have a PTIN.

CHAPTER 2

INCOME

"Never depend on a single income. Make investments
to create a second source"

-Warren Buffett

Most people think of a monthly rent check from a tenant or cash when it comes to income. Yes, that is the most common form, but there are other rental income types and different ways to record them. There are five primary forms of income for a rental property:

- **Advanced rent**. Rent paid in advance of the respective month must still be recorded as rental income when received even if the corresponding month is not in the current year. For example, if a tenant signs a lease in December and the Landlord asks for three months advance rent, the three months of rent would be income in December of the current year. Advanced rent covers rent if the tenant leaves early without notice.

- **Canceling a lease**. If your tenant pays a fee for early termination of their lease, you will have to record that income in the month you received it, regardless of when the tenant leaves.

- **Expenses paid by tenant**. If the tenant pays any of your expenses, those expenses are considered rental income. To deduct the expenses as rental expenses, you have to record the income. For example, the tenant's monthly rent is $900, and the water heater stops working when you are out of town. The tenant pays the cost for a new one amounting to $800. In the following month, you would only collect $100 in rent, and the $800 would also be considered income. Also, you would record the $800 as a deductible expense.

- **Security deposit**. Believe it or not, when you plan to return the deposit to the tenant at the end of the lease, it is not considered rental income. Instead, you must keep it in a separate account, and any interest accrued is taxable to the tenant. However, if the tenant does not live up to the terms of the lease, you can keep the security deposit, and it will be considered income.

- **Bartering**. If your tenant exchanges their services for rent, you have to include that as rental income. For example, a tenant who is a painter can paint a vacant apartment for you. If his standard fee is $500, you will record an income of $500 and maintenance expenses of $500. The tenant would reduce his rent payment to you by $500.

TIPS

- When charging discounted rent to a friend or family member, and the amount of rent is below market rate, your expenses are limited to the amount of rent you charge. So if you charge $100 a month and your expenses are $225, you are capped at a $100 deduction. So, no loss will be a deductible; you just break even.

- Security deposits cannot be used as an advancement of rent in most cases. When preparing the lease, be very clear in stating your intent for the security deposit. Make sure the lease specifies that you'll only return the security deposit if the tenant meets the terms of the lease. Advanced payments are kept regardless if the tenant adheres to the terms of the lease.

- If your tenant has unpaid rent, you cannot claim a deduction. The IRS knows that you should not pay taxes on rental income that is owed. In turn, the loss of income is not an additional expense to your actual expenses.

CHAPTER 3

EXPENSES

" Beware of little expenses. A small leak will sink a great ship"
- Benjamin Franklin

Here we will cover the fifteen categories of expenses found on Schedule E. Some investors will have expenses in all fifteen categories, and some may have only a few. It is essential, however, to know what's included in all of the categories. This way, you can ensure that you don't leave any money on the table as you conduct your real estate activities throughout the year.

Okay, let's get back to Cynthia and Michael.

LINE 5: ADVERTISING

As Cynthia approached the Schedule E expenses section, Michael wondered why she asked him about advertising when he explicitly told her he owned an investment property. Michael politely interjected, wondering if he had made the right decision in trying a new accountant. Cynthia chuckled and explained to him that "advertising is not just commercials or billboards, but any expense incurred for the purpose of getting your business known to potential customers" or, in Michael's case, "tenants." Therefore, the 'For Rent' signs and listings Michael paid to secure his current tenants are considered advertising costs. Michael's eyes started to flicker a little. "Do you mean to tell me the ads I placed on letsrenta.com were deductible?" he asked. Cynthia explained that "many real estate professionals and other entrepreneurs don't realize things like business cards, on-line or off line advertisements, billboards, For Rent signs, and so on are considered advertising expenses."

In their discussion, Cynthia learned that Michael spent the first six months of the time he owned his three-family home actively looking for a tenant. Based on this information, she determined that he could have used the additional deductions. Good thing Cynthia took the time to go over everything. After explaining the advertising deduction and ensuring that Michael did not miss any other potential expenses, they moved on.

TIPS

- In order to be considered a deductible advertising expense, one must have paid for an actual advertisement in a public forum. Word of mouth does not count!

- Being part of a local landlord association in your state or city can be advertising if they allow you to post your rental in a directory. The cost of that membership can be advertising if they enable that directory feature.

- Even if you had to make improvements or extensive repairs, the IRS insists that you are not allowed expenses if your rental property was vacant for a year or more. The IRS view is if it is not listed or marketed "For Rent," it is your second home and not a rental. That is a more complex topic, and we will not cover that in this book. Nonetheless, the point is to prove that you are actively marketing your units even if it is not ready to rent. Real estate developers do it all the time.

LINE 6: AUTO AND TRAVEL

As a real estate professional, auto and travel are your "bread and butter." If you stand still, you're losing money, so you must always be on the go. Unfortunately, most real estate professionals overlook expenses for auto and travel. Melissa did not keep any records of her auto and travel. Still, she drove to many open houses, traveled to see her lawyer, met inspectors, visited properties, attended closings, and took countless trips to the hardware store in the first weeks of her purchase. To qualify for auto and travel deductions, the IRS requires you to keep track of your start and endpoints, the purpose of the trip, mileage, and travel date. Melissa was becoming overwhelmed by all of these terms. She knew she would not remember what she needed to keep records for or consistently keep up tracking all of this on her own. Carlos understood this feeling of confusion because many people are unaware of what they need to do. He gave Melissa the following tips to get the most out of her auto and travel expenses.

WHENEVER POSSIBLE, AUTOMATE

Are you tech-savvy? If so, there is an app for that. Apps can have different features, but the main features to look for are automatically tracking your travel with one touch, storing your travel data, and providing reports. There are some excellent free and paid apps that can track your travel expenses and miles, such as:

- QuickBooks for Small Business
- MileIQ
- Everlance
- Trip log

Refer to each app for pricing and usage information. Oh, and if there is a fee, it's a deduction.

Not tech-savvy? No problem! Get a notebook and write down your travels. Keep an eye on where you went and how it relates to your real estate activity, and of course, keep track of the miles. The first thing you need to understand is that you can either deduct the actual expenses you paid or the standard mileage rate, not both and in some instances, you are required to use a particular method. Confused yet? No worries, we'll explain.

You must use the actual rate method if you use more than four vehicles simultaneously in your rental activity. So if you have four or more trucks you use to pick up your tenants' garbage, you must use actual expenses.

You can only use the standard mileage rate method if:

- You owned the vehicle and used the mileage rate in the first year you used the vehicle for your real estate services.

- You leased the vehicle and used the mileage rate for the entire lease period. You cannot switch back and forth. Melissa was shocked. She had no idea she had to pick one. She intended on taking the IRS mileage rate and her auto insurance, fuel cost, and even that costly repair to the transmission.

Let us show you why the approach you use to determine your mileage deduction is so important in calculating your overall deduction. Carlos pointed out the following chart to show Melissa, and she was even more shocked at the difference the different methods produced (See chart 1).

Chart 1

Miles Breakdown	1st Qtr	2nd Qtr	3rd Qtr	4th Qtr	Yearly Total
Total miles	3,844	3,955	3,995	3,548	15,342
Business miles	1,844	2,584	2,251	1,548	8,227
Percentage of Business Use	48%	65%	56%	44%	54%

Calculate Mileage Deduction	1st Qtr	2nd Qtr	3rd Qtr	4th Qtr	Yearly Total
Mileage rate: (This rate changes each year)	0.57	0.57	0.57	0.57	0.57
Business miles	1,844	2,584	2,251	1,548	8,227
Mileage Rate Amount	$1,051	$1,472	$1,283	$882	$4,689

Chart 1 Continued

Actual Expense	1st Qtr	2nd Qtr	3rd Qtr	4th Qtr	Yearly Total
Gasoline	$360	$384	$396	$420	$1,560
Oil	$65	$65	$65	$65	$260
Repairs	$250	$100	$2,500	$0	$2,850
Insurance	$450	$450	$450	$450	$1,800
Vehicle registration	$0	$0	$75	$0	$75
Licenses	$0	$0	$15	$0	$15
Lease fee	$0	$0	$0	$350	$350
Total actual expenses	$1,125	$999	$3,501	$1,285	$6,910
Percentage of business use	48%	65%	56%	44%	54%
Actual Expenses Amount	$540	$649	$1,960	$565	$3,731

Chart 1 Continued

Tax Deduction Summary	
Mileage rate amount	$4,731
Actual expense amount	$3,726

Carlos's chart clearly showed Melissa how the deduction is based on the number of miles driven for business regardless if you use your actual expenses or not. Carlos made it easy for her to follow the steps too. Here, try it:

Step 1: Divide your total business miles by your total miles to get a ratio.

Step 2: Take your business miles and multiply them by the standard mileage rate.

Step 3: Calculate your total actual expenses. Then multiply the amount by the business use ratio from Step 1.

Step 4: Your deduction is the higher of the two. Don't forget, though, if you lease your car, whatever method you use (actual vs. mileage), you are locked into that method for the life of the vehicle.

TIPS

- Get an app to record your miles and actual expenses. Time is money, and technology helps you save time. People did not stop buying disposable cameras because they do not work; technology saved you time to take the picture [with your phone].

- If you are recording by hand, the elements you need to keep are as follows:

  » Who did you go to meet for this trip ? *The who* can sometimes be a vendor like Staples or Home Depot, for example.

  » What did you do or talk about? Sometimes you are not meeting anyone, so keep the receipt that covers this element. The receipt is self-explanatory.

  » Where did you travel to confirm business use? If you use one of the apps we have listed above, they will capture this element.

- Keep a copy of the receipts of your actual expenses (e.g., airplane travel to annual landlord convention and meals).

Whether you use the standard or actual auto

expenses, you can always expense your tolls and parking costs separately from auto and travel by putting it with *other expenses.*

LINE 7: CLEANING AND MAINTENANCE

As a landlord, it is in your best interest to make sure your investment property is in excellent condition to attract and keep good tenants. State and local laws also require you to make sure your rental units are safe for tenants. Therefore, regular maintenance is a part of the cost of owning a rental property and may be expensed in the year it is performed. Upkeep of fixtures such as furnaces, boilers, and other appliances and external structures such as walls, grass, and sidewalks are considered qualified maintenance expenses and can be expensed over time.

As Cynthia educated Michael on cleaning and maintenance expenses for his three-family rental, he became excited. When he purchased the home two years ago, the previous owner had some hardships, and the home required some work to get the units ready for new tenants. Michael didn't have the time to do the job, so he hired a cleaning service. After work each evening, he would check on the progress of the unit. The total cost of the cleaning service was $2,000, and because the units were being prepared for rental use, Michael now realized he could deduct the total amount of these expenses on his amended returns. Michael was also able to deduct the mileage from driving to and from the rental property.

During his second year as Landlord, one of Michael's tenants suddenly moved due to a job relocation, and unfortunately for him, the tenant left the unit in shambles. This time, Michael decided to clean himself with the help of a couple of his buddies. While they were cleaning the unit, Michael decided to clean the gutters and sewer lines to avoid any potential issues during winter. Cynthia explained to Michael that he was "able to deduct the cost of the cleaning supplies and equipment he purchased to clean the unit this time around, too." During their discussion, Michael mentioned that he purchased a new water heater as a "few tenants had complained that the shower water was cold." He was not sure if this purchase was considered a repair or maintenance. To his surprise, Cynthia explained that "this expense was neither, but was actually an improvement." Unlike repairs and maintenance, which the IRS allows taxpayers to deduct in total in the current year, improvements have to be depreciated (a fancy term for deducted over time) over a period of five years. While Cynthia planned on explaining depreciation in more detail, she came to Line 18 on Schedule E and took the opportunity to give Michael a quick lesson.

IS IT MAINTENANCE, REPAIR, OR IMPROVEMENT

According to the IRS, an expense is an improvement if it meets the following criteria:

- It makes a long-term asset better than it was originally.

- It restores the asset to operating condition.

- It makes the asset into a new use.

On the other hand, repair and maintenance expenses do not necessarily extend an asset's useful life. Repairs typically fix a broken piece of your property, bringing it back to its original condition. Maintenance typically refers to activities that keep your property from deteriorating.

TIPS

- If you have to repeat the same project the following year, then most likely the project is deductible as maintenance expenses.

- It is best to put any repairs with one-time costs of $100 or less under maintenance; all others go to repairs on Line 14.

LINE 8: COMMISSIONS

Searching for the right rental property and tenants can be an arduous task, and sometimes, you need help from an expert. Three years ago, when Michael decided to venture into real estate investing, he was very green to the field. Like most people who purchase a home, Michael used a real estate agent to help him with the process. Usually, the buyer doesn't pay commission, but in this deal, he did.

After almost a year of searching, Michael found his current home. The realtor's fee was based on a percentage of the home's selling price, which Michael paid as part of his closing costs. While the realtor's fee is a commission, this type of commission is not deductible by the IRS. According to the IRS, the commissions paid to a Realtor before owning the property are considered part of the acquisition cost. These costs are required to be included in the purchase cost and depreciated over the property's life. Adding the commission to the home's purchase price increases your basis in the property, and in turn, reduces any gains when you may ultimately have to pay capital gains taxes (tax geek talk for, it helps you pay fewer taxes). Michael happened to have some of his home purchase documents with him, and they were able to review his prior two years of returns. He and Cynthia noticed that the commissions were appropriately included in the purchase price and were being depreciated over the correct 27.5-year life for an investment property.

Michael and Cynthia continued reviewing the commission's line, where he went on to explain how he had such a great experience with the realtor that he also used her to help him find tenants. As is typical with most Realtor fees, Michael paid the realtor the equivalent of one month's rent to find both of his tenants. Because the commission is after the purchase and directly related to renting the unit out, Cynthia made sure that Michael actually took the deduction for this second commission type. However, when reviewing Michael's return, she noticed there were no expenses in the commission expense line. Cynthia reviewed the depreciation expense worksheet for the corresponding year. There it was—the $2,400 realtor's fee being depreciated over 27.5 years, or in other words, an $87.27 deduction for the next 27.5 years. Cynthia corrected Michael's amended return, reflecting the full expense in the correct year.

Michael and Cynthia were making progress. Not only did Michael feel more comfortable with the amount of money he was going to receive back, and he also felt better because he now understood why. After making the corrections on the commission expense line, Cynthia and Michael moved on to insurance.

TIPS

- When it is time to sell the property, you get to expense out all of the commission you have not amortized. It is like the gift that keeps on giving, as we will show you in the Depreciation and Depreciation Recapture discussions

- If you plan to sell and want to lower your capital gains tax, have the unused commission be part of the capital gains calculation, reducing your taxes. Ask your tax professional for more advice on this topic.

LINE 9: INSURANCE

As a homeowner, whether for investment or personal purposes, your home is one of your biggest assets, and as such, you must protect it. Unfortunately, protecting your property for your personal use does not get you a deduction. Still, if you are in the rental property business, the IRS sees the cost of homeowner's insurance as a reasonable, ordinary, and necessary part of renting your property. Cynthia reviewed Michael's homeowner's insurance policy. She noted the original closing date of the house was March of last year, at which time Michael paid $1,800 for a homeowner's insurance policy through the period ending March of the current year. Reviewing the prior year's return Michael brought with him, the previous preparer incorrectly took the full $1,800 deduction instead of allocating the policy between the prior year and the current year. Cynthia performed the following calculation to determine the correct allocation of insurance expense to the correct period (See chart 2):

Chart 2.1

$1,800 / 12 = $150	Monthly expense
$150 / 3 units = $50 x 2 rental units = $100	Portion of monthly expense related to rental units
$100 x 10 = $1,000	Expense for March through December Prior year.
$100 x 2 = $200	Expense for January through February Current year.

Based on Cynthia's calculation, Michael's previous preparer deducted too much for insurance expenses; $200. While this is minimal, to keep accurate records, Cynthia made the respective adjustment on Michael's prior year amended return.

Meanwhile, on the other side of town, Carlos was

having a similar discussion with Melissa. As part of his explanation of mortgage interest paid to banks, Carlos explained Line 9 of Schedule E, related to mortgage insurance premiums. "You can treat the amounts you paid during the tax year for qualified mortgage insurance as home mortgage interest," he explained to Melissa. The insurance must be connected with home acquisition debt (the debt you incurred to buy the house), and the insurance contract must have been issued after the purchase of the property. Melissa's eyes glazed over. "What is mortgage insurance? And why in the world should I pay insurance on something if I already have it secured with my property?" she asked. "That is a great point, Melissa," Carlos said. "Mortgage insurance premium (MIP) is an insurance policy used in FHA loans. The FHA assesses either an upfront mortgage insurance premium (UFMIP) at the time of closing or an annual MIP that is calculated every year and paid in twelve installments." "Oh," Melissa said. "Then, in short, the bank doesn't trust me if I can't put 20 percent down?" "Not really," replied Carlos with a chuckle. FHA-insured loans require a small amount of cash to close a loan. As a result, all borrowers must pay a MIP to insure the lender against loss if they default on the mortgage. While there are ways to avoid PMI (Private Mortgage Insurance) with conventional loans, there is no way to avoid MIP on FHA loans.

TIPS

- Review your HUD 1 before and after closing to confirm if you paid points. Have your lawyer or lender review the amounts you paid to make sure points were not included with another closing cost. Have them point out the points to you so you can see them with your own eyes.

- Confirm if you are subject to mortgage insurance premiums with your lender and how they were paid. If you prepaid the full twelve months at closing on Schedule E, you can take the full deduction. If you are going to pay your first year in monthly installments, you can only deduct what was paid in the current year.

- For FHA loans, the insurance is called MIP; however, it is called PMI for a conventional loan. The good thing with conventional if you put more than 20% down can avoid PMI; that is not the case with FHA.

LINE 10: LEGAL AND OTHER
PROFESSIONAL FEES

Joking with Cynthia, Michael mentioned that while he loves being a landlord, one thing he realized was that he has never had to go to court as much in his life! His first experience was when he, unfortunately, had to sue one of his tenants. While they paid the rent on time, they repeatedly violated the lease by having loud parties on the weekdays until 2 a.m. and an unauthorized pet.

The second time Michael was in court, he successfully sued the city to defend his right to improve the property. This happened before, but his prior accountant did not report the return's expense, saying the amount was so large it would raise red flags. Cynthia got a kick out of Michael's joke because she sees new homeowners' excitement all the time until they sign on the dotted line and everything is on them. But in the end, it all works out. Cynthia looked over all of Michael's legal expenses and asked him what each expense was for. Michael provided detailed explanations for each expense, and with each explanation, Cynthia placed an E or a C next to the expense. Michael was eager for her to finish explaining what she was doing. The expenses were as follows (See Chart 3.1):

Chart 3.1

E = Expenses in the current year   C = Capitalized over 27.5 years

Paid to	Amount	C/E Description
Real Deal Legal	$250	E - Review lease and provide advice to remove the tenant for breach of contract.
JJ Tax Service	$350	E - Prepare real estate value return for FL property.
Real Deal Legal	$2,500	C - Defend and protect title of property from Big Box Corp.
Real Deal Legal	$1,000	C - Recover a section of land that was parceled incorrectly.
Real Deal Legal	$790	C - Cost for lawyer to petition city to develop/improve new section of land.
Real Deal Legal	$1,500	E - Total cost of legal advice for the year on the loud tenants.
Total Expenses	**$6,390**	

Chart 3.1 Continued

Summary:	
E—Expenses	$2,100
C—Capitalize	$4,290
Life of property	27.5 yr.
Deduction in Year 1.	$156

Tax Deduction	
E—Expenses	$2,100
C—Capitalize expenses	$156
Total Tax Deduction	$2,256

Cynthia explained that, per tax law, Michael could "only expense the cost of legal advice and the preparation of tax forms related to the real estate property." He could not fully deduct legal fees paid or incurred to defend or protect the property title, recover property, or develop or improve it. Instead, he had to capitalize these fees over the life of the property. The life of a rental property is 27.5 years. Michael was happy that the expense wasn't disregarded, but he was a little confused about what would happen to the capitalized expenses in the future. Cynthia said he would get a deduction of $156 for the next 27.5 years, and if he sells the property before then, the balance at the date of sale would be added to the cost of the property (fewer taxes paid on the sale). She gave the following example:

Chart 4.1

Selling price of home in Current year	250,000
Adjusted Cost basis of property	153,510 (A+B)
Gain on sale	96,490
Capitalized expense start	4,290

Year 1.	(156)
Year 2.	(156)
Year 3.	(156)
Year 4.	(156)
Year 5.	(156)

Capitalized expense balance at current year	3,510 (A)
Adjusted Cost of property at year of sale	150,000 (B)

Michael understood now. The money was not lost but just pushed forward in $156 increments. And if he didn't use it all, it reduced the gain on the sale or increased the loss on the sale. He finally felt like he knew what was going on.

TIPS

- Try to take advantage of the legal deduction by seeking legal advice and preparation of forms when possible knowing that you can expense them.

- Record the purpose of the legal expenses so you can keep track if it is capitalized or expensed.

- Amounts paid to facilitate the acquisition or production of real or personal property must also be capitalized. Facilitative costs include items such as architectural, engineering, environmental, or inspection services related to specific properties, brokers, or appraisers' fees, and services provided by a qualified intermediary in a like-kind exchange

LINE 11: MANAGEMENT FEES

Michael was happy he and Cynthia were making their way through Schedule E at a steady pace. Now almost halfway through the schedule, Cynthia arrived at the management fee expense line. Knowing Michael had a three-family home in which he lived, Cynthia was about to skip this section, but something told her to take her time and investigate further just in case. "By any chance, did you ever hire anyone to run your property?" she asked. Michael looked a little confused, so Cynthia asked if he hired anyone to do any of the following:

- Regularly fix tenants' maintenance and repair issues

- Show vacant units to prospective renters

- Collect rent from tenants

Michael thought about it and told Cynthia that he traveled a lot for his job in the second year of owning the home, and since he was not home often, he hired a company to manage the property and handle tenant issues while away for long durations. Michael dug into his bag of receipts and documents he brought along with him and saw that he had an invoice from Columbia Property Managers for $1,200. Cynthia checked Michael's prior year return and saw this item was not included, so she added it to the respective line of the amended return.

TIPS

Instead of paying a company to manage your property in this tech-driven world, you can automate this function using a property management application such as one offered by Apartment.com (formerly called Cozy. These apps can automate the following functions:

- Rent income collection

- Rental applications

- Renter screening tools

LINE 12: MORTGAGE INTEREST

Melissa may not know much about taxes, but she was certain of one thing—her mortgage payment was deductible, just not sure how much. Looking at what the bank said she paid in interest, Melissa was excited, but she was also worried that there was more to it after all she has learned from Carlos. She was excited because the amount was more than $8,000, and she was certain it would translate to a big refund no matter what; however, she felt it was lower than expected. Being in the office with Carlos made her comfortable because he made things easy to understand, so she asked what she thought was a senseless question. With her head down, looking at her mortgage statement, she asked: "I'm not sure if I'm asking something that is senseless, but can I deduct mortgage interest, and why is the number lower than what I paid per month?" Carlos smiled. "That's not a senseless question. It's a concern of many, and honestly, you must understand the foundation of mortgage interest." Melissa smiled as she lifted her head from the tax papers. She was happy that she did not look like a novice, and her questions were common. Carlos kindly asked that she put the tax document on the desk to talk about it. "The form you had in your hand is called a Form 1098," he began.

WHAT IS A 1098?

If you paid $600 or more of mortgage interest (including certain points and mortgage insurance premiums) during the year on any one mortgage, you generally would receive a Form 1098 or a similar statement from the mortgage holder. You will receive the statement if you pay interest to a person (including a financial institution or cooperative housing corporation) in the course of that person's trade or business. The statements for each year should be sent to you by January 31st of the following year. A copy of this form will also be sent to the IRS. The statement will show the total interest you paid during the year, any mortgage insurance premiums you paid, and if you purchased a main home during the year. It also will show the deductible points paid during the year, including seller-paid points. (see number three below). As a general rule, Form 1098 will include only points you can fully deduct in the year paid.

However, certain points not included on Form 1098 also may be deductible, either in the year paid or over the life of the loan. Looking back up at Melissa, Carlos said, "Since you purchased the property in the year this 1098 was issued, it looks like there are more payments that were not listed on this form. There is more money out there for us." The words were like a hug from her mother. Melissa was happy to know she had more deductions in addition to the $8,000.

There are four things you must be aware of with mortgage interest deductions:

- Debt secured by a home. You can deduct your home mortgage interest only if your mortgage is a secured debt. Secured debt is one in which you sign a document, such as a mortgage, deed of trust, or land contract that makes your ownership in a qualified home, security for payment of the debt. In case of default, it provides that your home could satisfy the debt and is recorded or is otherwise perfected under any state or local law that applies.

- Debt not secured by a home. Debt is not secured by your home if it is secured solely because of a lien on your general assets or if it is a security interest that attaches to the property without your consent (such as a mechanic's lien or judgment lien). In other words, when you take out a home mortgage, your home becomes collateral to protect the interests of the lender. If you cannot pay the debt, the lender can use your home to satisfy the debt. In this book, the term "mortgage" will refer to secured debt.

- Points. The term, points, is used to describe certain charges paid or treated as paid by a borrower to obtain a home mortgage. Points may also be called loan origination fees, maximum loan charges, loan discount, or discount points. What you need to know about points is: A borrower is treated as paying any points that a home seller pays for the borrower's mortgage. You generally cannot deduct the full amount of points in the year paid. Because points are prepaid interest, you generally deduct them, by rate, over the mortgage's life.

- Mortgage insurance premiums. Well, Carlos explained this earlier as part of the insurance deduction. Look back at Line 9 about insurance.

Once Melissa heard she could not deduct the full amount of points in the year paid, her heart dropped. She knew from her lender that the points were close to 3 percent of the sale price, and now she could not deduct it all. "There is still hope, Melissa," Carlos said as if he knew she was thinking of the 3 percent in points. "There is a way to deduct all of the points you paid in the tax year you paid them in, but you must meet all the following tests," he said. They are as follows:

- Your loan is secured by your main home. (Your main home is the one you ordinarily live in most of the time.)

- Paying points is a common business practice in the area where the loan is made.

- The amount of points paid is not more than what is generally charged in that area.

- You use the cash method of accounting. This means you report income in the year you receive it and deduct expenses in the year you pay them. Most individuals use this method.

- The points are not paid in the place of another closing cost (see settlement statement) such as appraisal fees, inspection fees, title fees, attorney fees, and property taxes. That means if you paid an additional one percent in points to cover title fees, you could not take the full deduction for the points.

- The money you provided at or before closing, plus any points the seller paid, were at least as much as the points charged. The funds you provided are not required to have been applied to the points; they just have to be the same or more. They can include a down payment, an escrow deposit, earnest money, and other funds you paid at or before closing for any purpose. You cannot have borrowed these funds from your lender or mortgage broker.

- You use your loan to buy or build your main home.

- The points were computed as a percentage of the principal amount of the mortgage.

- The amount is clearly shown on the settlement statement (such as the Settlement Statement, Form Closing Disclosures (CD) as points charged for the mortgage. The points may be shown as paid from either your funds or the seller's funds.

"Yes!" Melissa said. She met all nine tests and could take a deduction of an additional $3,090. Carlos was glad she met all the tests, as most people do. The one test that can make or break a client, which Carlos has learned over his years of service, is the test I, above. Sometimes, it is not on the CD, or it is on the CD but not shown clearly because it is hidden in other costs.

TIPS

- Make sure you have the Form 1098 or the equivalent to prepare your taxes. That is your proof of interest paid.

- Did you know you can deduct mortgage interest from a family member or friend as long as the file is Form 1098?

LINE 13: OTHER INTEREST

Cynthia reviewed Michael's expenses worksheet that he provided and saw a total of $101,112 in improvements. She recalled that his wages were only $90,000 and knew it was one of two things: either he had a rich uncle or took out a second loan. Cynthia took a look at his Form 1098 and noticed that his interest paid more than doubled from what she saw in prior years. She showed Michael where on his CD and his Form 1098 he could find the information for the second mortgage or line of equity. Michael was well aware of the mortgage interest deduction but was not clear on the treatment of this second mortgage and the line of equity he took out to improve the property. Cynthia always explained to her clients the complex rules and regulations of using their property's equity to improve the property. "Congratulations, Michael," she said after reviewing the new CD and 1098. "You were able to leverage your property's equity to improve it. This is a true gift, but I would like to make sure you qualify for the full deduction of the additional mortgage interest."

Michael made sure he consulted his prior tax preparer before he made this big move to confirm he would be able to write off everything from the cost of the improvements to the new monthly payment. Cynthia indicated that he should be okay but wanted to make sure he was aware of the tax rules and regulations to confirm he was audit-proof. There were two main tests they needed to cover:

- You use the mortgage to buy, build, or improve a home. A mortgage secured by a qualified home may be treated as home acquisition debt, even if you do not actually use the proceeds to buy, build, or substantially improve the home. This applies in the following situations:

  » You buy your home within ninety days before or after the date you take out the mortgage. The home acquisition debt is limited to the home's cost, plus the cost of any substantial improvements.

» You build or improve your home and take out the mortgage before the work is completed. The home acquisition debt is limited to the amount of the expenses incurred within twenty-four months before the mortgage date.

» You build or improve your home and take out the mortgage within 90-days after the work is completed. The home acquisition debt is limited to the amount of the expenses incurred within the period beginning twenty-four months before the work is completed and ending on the mortgage date.

• Substantial improvement. An improvement is substantial if it:

» Adds to the value of your home

» Prolongs your home's useful life or

» Adapts your home to new uses

Cynthia explained that substantial improvement is the make-or-break question. Repairs that maintain your home in good condition, such as repainting your home, are not substantial improvements. However, if you paint your home as part of a renovation that substantially improves your qualified home, you can include the painting costs in the improvement cost. The cost of building or substantially improving a qualified home includes the costs to acquire real property and building materials, fees for architects and design plans, and required building permits.

TIPS

Get the most out of the other interest deduction.

- The term home acquisition debt is a financial debt taken to construct, improve, or purchase a property.

- Be sure to separate the loan amount to substantially improve the property from payments for repairs to get more bang for your buck.

- Be sure to bring the new CD for the new or second mortgage to your tax preparer.

- Remember, you can also fully deduct points in the year paid on a loan to improve your main home if you meet the tests A-I that we talked about in the points section. (See Line 12 on points).

LINE 14: REPAIRS AND IMPROVEMENT

Melissa's appointment was going better than she ever expected. She gained so much knowledge that she felt she'd be so prepared it would be unfair next year. She felt she had a handle on the expense of the repairs. She purchased a dilapidated property, and the loan included a 203K rehab portion that allotted $65,701 to repair the property. As Melissa looked at Carlos reviewing the spreadsheet she prepared for him, she could not help noticing his disposition, as he was awfully fidgety. He tapped his pencil near the number, circled it, went to his calculator, and quickly typed in something, then looked at Melissa and said, "The amount of repairs you have is way too high." Melissa was surprised. She made sure she totaled her invoices correctly for the five months' worth of repairs at $65,701.

After about five seconds of silence as if it were a Wild West showdown, Melissa calmly said, "I have the invoices and receipts for everything." Carlos asked to see the invoices and receipts. While going through her receipts and invoices and bundling them into two groups, he started to explain why the amount for repairs was too high. Commonly, an expense for repairing or maintaining your rental property may be deducted in the current year if you are not required to capitalize the expense, he said. On the other hand, expenses you pay to improve your property must be capitalized, or in other words, allocating the cost of the expense over the life of the items rather than taking the full expenses in the year paid. An expense is considered an improvement if it results in any of the following:

- Betterment to your property. Expenses that may result in a betterment to your property include expenses for fixing a pre-existing defect or condition, enlarging or expanding your property, or increasing the capacity, strength, or quality of your property.

- Restores your property. Expenses that may be for restoration include expenses for replacing a substantial structural part of your property, repairing damage to your property after you properly adjusted the basis of it as a result of a casualty loss, or rebuilding your property to a like-new condition.

• Adapts your property to a new or different use. Expenses that may be for adaptation include expenses for altering your property to a use that is not consistent with the intended, ordinary use when you began renting the property.

After a moment, Carlos blurts out, "It's $2,651." "What is that?" Melissa asked, totally confused. "That is your repair deduction this year," Carlos answered. Melissa was speechless. Actually, the words that came to mind were unprofessional for this book. So she took a deep breath and slowly asked, "Can you give me an explanation of how you got to that number?" "Sure," said Carlos as he printed out a sheet for her to review. The expenses you capitalize for improving your property have to be depreciated over the improvement's useful life as follows:

Chart 5.1

Additions/ Improvements	Useful Life: 27.5 Years
Bedroom(s)	$3,151

Bathroom(s)	$4,151
Deck	$2,541
Garage	$1,548
Porch	$1,684
Patio	$1,998
New roof	$7,893
Storm windows, doors	$984
Septic system	$1,511
Water heater	$850
Built-in appliances	$2,697
Kitchen modernization	$6,874
Flooring	$5,984
Wall-to-wall carpeting	$3,449
Total Additions	**$45,315**

Lawn and Grounds	Useful Life: 15 Years
Driveway	$5,418
Fence	$6,547
Retaining wall	$2,359
Sprinkler system	$3,411
Total Lawn and Grounds	$17,735
Total Improvements	**$63,050**

Chart 5.1 Continued

Repairs	
Front and back door	$1,500
Back and front steps	$1,151
Total Repairs	**$2,651**
Total 203k Loan	**$65,701**

"Ahhh, I see," Melissa said. "This is making a lot more sense. So if I understand correctly, if I improve the structure of my property, it is not a repair?" "You are a fast one," Carlos said with a big smile. It always felt good when a client began to understand.

TIPS

- Separate the costs of repairs and improvements and keep accurate records. You will need to know the cost of improvements when you sell or depreciate your property.

- List and place the amount(s) you paid accordingly as done in the list above

- Remember, a repair fixes the problem and is a deductible expense. An Improvement replaces the item and makes it better than it was prior. Improvements are capitalized over their useful life. ((See depreciation Line 18)

Line 15: Supplies

The appointment was going well, and Melissa was feeling increasingly confident in Carlos. As they continued their meeting, Melissa even took a stab at helping Carlos determine her supplies deduction. "If I'm not mistaken, these would be considered supplies expenses," Melissa said, presenting the following receipts.

Chart 6.1

Item	Amount
Screwdriver set	$20

Screws	$10
Cleaning supplies	$150
Garden hose	$20
Plunger	$5
Rental applications	$20

Melissa incurred all the expenses for items used while performing routine maintenance and business tasks throughout the year. When she and Carlos went through the remainder of the receipts, they determined Melissa's supply deduction for the year was $225. Carlos explained to Melissa that "due to the short-term nature of these expenses, the total amount would be deducted in the current year." Melissa was pleased.

TIPS

- Record common supplies that are often overlooked, such as garbage bags, light bulbs, and receipt books to record rental payments.

- Don't forget to keep your receipts!

Line 16: Taxes

Melissa's Schedule E was almost complete. As she looked at Carlos' computer screen, she noticed an error. "That's not correct, Carlos," she said. "What's wrong?" he asked, surprised. "My property taxes are $13,000 per my property tax card. I am sure of that, but you have only $6,000 for taxes," she said. "Oh, I see," Carlos said. "I always feel that I should explain the taxes line before I explain why the number is different." Carlos explained that deductible real estate taxes are generally "any state, local, or foreign taxes on real property collected for the general public welfare." The charge must be uniform against all real property in the jurisdiction at a like rate. Many states and counties also impose local benefit taxes on property improvements, such as assessments for streets, sidewalks, and sewer lines. "You cannot deduct local benefit taxes," Carlos said. "However, you can increase the cost basis of your property by the amount of the assessment. Local benefits taxes (improvements to the property, such as assessments for streets, sidewalks, and sewer lines) are deductible if they are for maintenance or repair or interest charges related to those benefits."

"That's a lot to take in," Melissa said. Carlos chuckled and said, "Okay. To keep it short, taxes assessed by your municipality that are assessed on your property are deductible. Still, a tax imposed for your municipality's benefit is not deductible and added to the purchase price of the property." Melissa understood now. Carlos continued, "But the reason your amount is $6,000 is that a portion of your monthly mortgage payment goes into an escrow account, and periodically, the lender pays your real estate taxes out of the account to the local government for that period. You can only deduct the amount paid out of the escrow account for the year, not what is on your tax card." He continued, "Secondly, per your Form 1098, where your interest is reported, it includes the amount paid for taxes as $12,000. However, since you live in 50% of the property and rent out 50%, we can only take the rental property portion on Schedule E, and the rest is deducted as an itemized deduction on Schedule A. Based on this, it looks like we have the right deduction." "Wow," Melissa responded, impressed and pleasantly surprised, "how do you accountants remember all of this?"

TIPS

- You can pay your fourth-quarter property taxes in the current year to get a bigger deduction.

- Know what local benefit and property taxes are. If you are ever audited, the auditor will examine it because it is often overlooked.

- The IRS Form 1098 should show the amount of property taxes you paid to the jurisdiction in the year. Do not confuse this with your property tax card, which shows the jurisdiction billed you for the year.

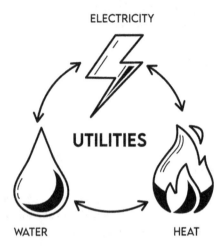

Line 17: Utilities

On the other side of town, Cynthia reviewed Michael's numbers perplexed. Cynthia raised her eyebrows and squinted as she looked over his numbers. "Is this number correct, Michael? Did you only pay $5,500 in utilities?" she asked. Michael thought that was a strange question. Could he have missed something? "Yeah, that's it," he said with uncertainty. "That seems very low for the number of units you have in the property," Cynthia said. She noticed Michael listed gas, water, electric, and heat, but she recalled him saying earlier that his county sewer system was all messed up.

"What about sewer?" she asked. Michael was quiet. She was right; he didn't know his sewer repairs qualified as utility expenses. Michael found the receipt, and they updated his prior and current year return for the expenses.

TIPS

Utilities is another one of the more straightforward lines on the return, so there is not much to go into here. The way to get the most out of this line is to keep track of the most common landlord-paid utilities:

- Water

- Sewer

- Heat

- Electricity

- Gas

- Oil

- Trash and Recycling

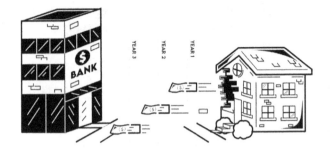

Line 18: Depreciation

"We are almost done, and we are getting to the sweet-and-sour expenses of accounting," Carlos said. "The sweet and sour?" Melissa chuckled, a little confused by the reference. "Yep, let me explain," Carlos said. "We'll start with the sweet. The cost you paid for the property is the largest expense you have in the year of purchase, but you can't take it all at once. You have to spread it over 27.5 years. However, over that time frame, it is the gift that keeps on giving because it is one of your largest deductions." Carlos grinned slyly. "But after I explain how much you can deduct each year compared to how much you paid originally, it may leave a sour taste." Melissa replied, "As much as I don't like the 'good news / bad news' method, please break it down slowly." Carlos explained, "See, the actual cost of a house, apartment building, or other rental property is not fully deductible in the year in which you pay for it. Instead of taking a deduction for the full $250,000 purchase price of your home, the IRS requires you to divide the cost evenly over 27.5 years." "Twenty-seven point five years? I don't even know where I'll be in two, five, or seven years, for that matter," Melissa said. "So tell me, what is the portion I get to deduct each year then?" "Good question," Carlos said. "But before I take you down that road, there are four points about depreciation I want you to know."

Generally, depreciation for rental property owners falls into the following categories:

- **5-Year Property:** Appliance and Equipment. Property, such as your stoves, refrigerators, equipment, and cars, are considered long-term property because they can be used for more than one year. Unlike your rental expenses that are not long-term, such as meals, travel expenses, landscaping, and insurance, and are fully deducted in the same year they're consumed.

- **7-Year Property:** Office Furniture and Fixtures. Property you use in connection with your rental activity, such as office furniture and fixtures, including desks, file cabinets, and safes.

- **15-Year Property:** Land Improvements consists of certain improvements made directly to the land or added to it to enhance the appearance and value of the land, such as shrubbery, fencing, sidewalk, and driveways.

- **27.5-Year Property:** Building and Structures. Real property is the structures attached to the land. You can depreciate any structure you use for your rental activity—apartment buildings, houses, swimming pools, parking lots, parking garages, and other facilities for your tenants. You can also depreciate structures you own and use for your rental activity, even though your tenants do not use them. For example, a building you use as your rental office or a storage shed where you keep maintenance equipment. Keep in mind you can only depreciate property that wears out, gets used up, or becomes outdated over time. Land—that is, the ground a building rests on and the surrounding area—can not be depreciated because it lasts forever for all practical purposes.

When you determine your depreciation deduction for a rental building or other structure, you cannot include the value of the land for tax purposes. You can only depreciate the cost of the building itself. Refer to your tax assessment card for the Land to Building ratio. Melissa was silent. Carlos could see her trying to process what he just said. "This was so enlightening and at the same time annoying because I paid $3,000 for new carpets, $800 for the stove, $300 for the refrigerator, and now you're saying I can only take a slice of the expenses I paid? Come on. This is so wrong," Melissa said. This is an issue Carlos and Cynthia see every tax season. Clients come in with a long list of expenses, but most of them are depreciable. "I got the sour taste now," Melissa said, slumping back in her chair. Carlos just nodded, understanding Melissa's frustration. "Well, I'm so ready for the sweetness right about now," she joked. "Well, the sweet is for at least the next five years or more," Carlos said. "You get the depreciation deduction for these expenses, and you didn't put out any additional cash. "For example, you bought the rental property for $250,000, and the value of the land is $50,000. You will depreciate $200,000 over 27.5 years for a yearly deduction of $7,273. "The only thing is when you sell the property, if you have a gain, you'll deal with another sour taste, but that is later down the line. I think you've had enough sour for today." (See depreciation recapture in the bonus chapter.) They both chuckled and moved on with the meeting.

Depreciation is a complex topic. Again, please consult a qualified tax professional to help you with this topic.

TIPS

- For each asset you depreciate, keep accurate records showing:

  » A description of the asset,

  » When and how you purchased the property,

  » The date you placed it in service, and

  » Its original cost.

- You can use our handy chart in the back of this book to see the life of some of the most common properties.

Line 19: Other Expenses

Carlos and Cynthia explained to their respective clients that there are so many other operating deductions for real estate professionals that it's difficult to cover them all because each real estate professional's situation is unique.

What Pocket Advisers suggest is that you familiarize yourself with the following:

Dues and Subscriptions. If your investment property is in a condo or co-op, the membership and association fees are deductible. Also, your local chamber of commerce or real estate civic or public service organization dues is deductible.

Education Expenses. Costs you incur to increase your knowledge, such as this book, attending real estate investment seminars, or taking educational courses related to your real estate investment, are deductible. The education expenses can include, but are not limited, to fees, tuition, and even the cost to travel to the course.

Gifts. That tenant who pays on time, keeps the property clean, and refers you to the best tenants deserves a gift. Why not buy him or her a bottle of wine or a gift card to a local store? Guess what? As long as the gift is $25 or less for each person per year, it is deductible.

Meals. There are two types of meals: Meals can be 50% deductible under the following scenarios Business Meeting: If you are looking to improve the curb appeal of your property and you decide to invite the contractor to the local coffee shop to talk terms, conditions, and of course, price, the cost of the food, drinks, and tips are deductible. However, the deduction is limited to 50 percent of the cost. Remember, with this type of meal, you must:

- Be accompanied by a new customer or vendor who you are trying to solicit

- You must discuss your rental activities.

Business Travel: The IRS figures that whether you're at home or away on a business trip, you have to eat; therefore, home meals ordinarily aren't deductible. Along the same lines, the IRS won't let you deduct all of your food expenses while traveling. Instead, you can deduct 50% of your meal expenses while on a business trip. There are two ways to calculate your meal expense deduction:

- You can keep track of your actual expenses.

- Use a daily rate set by the federal government.

TIPS

- Other expenses can be almost anything from homeowners association fees to home warranty costs you pay on equipment. Keeping records of everything is the key.

- A savvy investor can gain more tax savings by registering a trade name and obtaining a tax ID number to move some of the other expenses from Schedule E (passive income) to Schedule C (ordinary income). With Schedule E, you are subject to passive income limitations that do not apply to Schedule C. Speak to your tax advisor to see if this is a good fit for you.

- Unpaid Rent. Unpaid rent is not deductible unless you're using an accrual-based accounting system. For small landlords, this is seldom the case. You're likely using a cash-based system; therefore, unpaid rent is not deductible.

Wrapping Up

Having gone line by line through Schedule E, Michael and Melissa were 100 times more confident with their tax returns. They each walked out of the respective offices knowing everything was covered. We want you to feel the same. Now that you know what Michael and Melissa know, you can organize your expenses accordingly and have a good understanding of how to maximize your expenses to keep more money out of the hands of the government, legally. We warn you; this will lead to more income, a feeling of accomplishment, and lasting smiles on April 15th each year. You have been warned. Now that you've become an instant real estate professional, what will you do next?

BONUS

Depreciation Recapture

Fast-forward five years. Michael and Melissa have been loyal clients of Cynthia and Carlos and are pleased with the professional level of service they received over the years. Both of them have learned how to keep better records, and they've maximized their rental property deductions as a result.

In September, Melissa decided it was time to take a leap and purchase a four-family property. She found a deal she could not pass up and put her investment property on the market. It sold almost instantly with a gain of $100,000, and in December, she closed on her new property. When Melissa arrived at Carlos' office in February to have her current year's taxes done, she could not help thinking about the first year she met with him. How far have I come? she thought to herself. Remembering that first visit, Melissa knew exactly what to bring to the meeting. She was so excited to share the news about her new home with Carlos.

As she sat down and they came to the point of selling the prior investment property, Carlos had some bad news.

"You are going to have a sour taste in your mouth," Carlos said.

"Oh boy, not this again," Melissa said as she prepared for the news.

"You remember that deduction that keeps on going called depreciation?" Carlos asked.

"Oh, yeah," Melissa said. "I love depreciation. That extra $7,273 was great! Especially when the property started paying for itself."

"Well, now you may have to pay taxes on a portion or all of the depreciation that you took at your current ordinary income tax rate instead of your long-term capital gain," he said.

"What? You did not tell me about this," Melissa said. "I would've never taken that deduction if I knew I had to add it back and pay taxes on it. I need you to break this down to me step by step."

Carlos could see she was not happy and replied, "I know it sucks, but the way the tax law is written, you will still have to recapture depreciation expenses if you deducted it or not." Melissa slumped back into her chair to listen to the steps. "Okay, let's jump right in," Carlos said.

Step 1– Record the original purchase price of the asset. This price should include all costs paid to acquire the assets, such as taxes and commissions, if applicable.

Step 2 – Compute the depreciation expense that you took or that was allowed.

Step 3 – Subtract the taken or allowable depreciation expense from your original cost basis. This amount is your adjusted cost basis.

Step 4 – Record a number of your sales proceeds. This is your net amount after you pay any fees or commissions.

Step 5 – Subtract your adjusted cost basis from your sales proceeds. This is the amount of gain you have realized. A considerable depreciation expense can dramatically change the amount of tax you may have to pay on the sale.

Step 6– Compare your realized gain with your depreciation expense. The lower of these two figures is the amount the IRS considers to be the depreciation recapture.

Step 7– Treat the amount of your depreciation recapture as ordinary income and the remainder as a long-term capital gain.

"And to think, I felt I was going to pay taxes on just $100,000," Melissa said. "What if I had a loss? What would've happened? Would I still have to pay taxes on the $100,000?"

"Nope," Carlos said. "It's just if you have a gain so, you would've been okay."

"I should've sold at a loss," Melissa joked.

Keeping Records

Michael was talking to his friend at a bar, and he bragged about how good his accountant was. He was also able to give tax tips to his friends who owned rental properties. It made him feel proud to know he was working with the best. One night, his close friend Steven asked, Michael was talking to his friend at a bar, and he bragged about how good his accountant was. He was also able to give tax tips to his friends who owned rental properties. It made him feel proud to know he was working with the best. One night, his close friend Steven asked, "So how long did your accountant tell you to keep your records? My guy says don't worry about it and keep them for about two years." Michael was stuck. He had no idea. So he decided to show off his accountant to

Steven. "Let's ask the expert," he replied. As he called Cynthia, he was silently praying she'd picked up the phone. On the third ring, he heard her pleasant voice:

"Hello, Cynthia Lubin, CPA."

"Hello, Cynthia, this is Michael. How are you?" he said.

"I am doing fine, Michael; how are you?" she replied.

"I am good," Michael said. "I have a question. I am here with a friend, and he asked how long he should keep records for his rental property. Can you give us some guidance?"

"Sure I can, but do you have time? There are some main points to cover," Cynthia said.

"Yeah, we have time," Michael said, looking at Steven for approval. Steven nodded in approval.

"Okay, great," Cynthia said.

She continued, "First, keeping full and accurate records is vital to report your income and expenses properly, to support your deductions and credits, and to know the basis or adjusted basis of your home. These records would include your purchase contract and settlement papers, which prove you bought the property, or other objective evidence if you acquired it by gift, inheritance, or similar means. You should keep any receipts, canceled checks, and similar evidence for improvements or other additions and expenses." She paused for a second to make sure they understood.

"Okay, got it," Michael replied. "Secondly," Cynthia continued, "the way you keep records is up to you, but they must be clear and accurate and must be available to the IRS if requested. Always assume they will be needed."

"What if I keep them in a shoebox?" Michael asked.

"The old, trusty shoebox safe storage system." Cynthia chuckled. "You can do that, Michael, but remember, it must be clear, and over time, oxidation can make your records go blank, and poof! The deduction is gone if you have no other way of proving it."

"Good point," Michael said.

"Finally, you must keep your records for as long as they are important for meeting any provision of the federal tax law," Cynthia explained.

"Keep records that support an item of income, a deduction, or a credit appearing on a return until the period of limitations for the return runs out. This is generally three years from the date you filed the return. However, you must keep records relating to property improvement for longer than the period of limitations. Keep those records as long as they are important in figuring out the basis of the property. This means for as long as you own the property and one year after you dispose of it." Cynthia wrapped up her explanation.

"Wow, that is a long time," Michael said. He went on, "So let me get this straight. I keep records of income and expenses for three years after I file the return and keep records of the property's cost and improvement for one year after I sell the property. Or if I don't sell, forever." "Correct," Cynthia said.

"That is crazy. Why is the tax law like that?" Michael asked.

"Yes, it is a pain, but in the tax law, the taxpayer has the burden of proof that the income was received and expenses were incurred. The IRS just has to accuse you, but you have to prove your innocence," she said.

Steven and Michael finished the call with common

pleasantries and sat in disbelief at what they just heard. Steven looked at Michael and said, "I have to change accountants." They laughed.

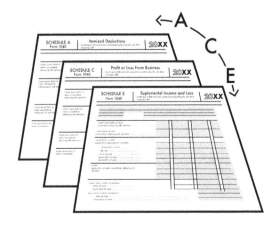

Schedules

There are different schedules for real estate transactions. This book is a quick guide for Schedule E only.

Schedule A versus Schedule E versus Schedule C: What's the Difference?

Schedule E: The IRS tax form used to calculate net income or loss from your passive activities. There are some rules and limitations on passive-activity income, which the form has the formulas built in to calculate. If you have a passive-activity loss, your deduction is limited to the amount of passive activity income. The outcome of the schedule will "flow-through" to your personal return and will be taxed along with all of your personal income items.

This guide is for real estate professionals who will file a Schedule E, which is for individuals who receive supplemental income such as royalties or income from a partnership or S-Corp. Still, the most common reason is for reporting rental income from a tenant. As this is not your primary business and you do not offer a range of services to tenants, the IRS does not consider you self-employed. Therefore, you do not have to file a Schedule C. You still must report all income and losses from your rental activities.

Schedule C: If you provide more than essential services (e.g., trash collection, utilities, basic maintenance) or are actively involved in the renting of space to tenants as your primary business, then you are considered self-employed and are required to file a Schedule C.

Schedule A: If you use any portion of your rental property as your personal residence, then you are required to allocate the related expenses between personal and business use. You can only deduct real estate taxes and mortgage interest expenses on the personal side.

The lines we discuss will appear on both schedules but keep in mind your participation level, so you use the correct schedule and, in turn, the correct treatment of your expenses. Now that we've explained the different schedules, there is another important concept every real estate professional should know.

The lines we discuss will appear on both schedules, but keep in mind your level of participation so you use the correct schedule and, in turn, the correct treatment of your expenses. Now that we've explained the different schedules, there is another important concept every real estate professional should know.

Passive versus Active Real Estate Professionals

The IRS has two classifications for real estate professionals: active or passive. If you are a passive real estate professional, you're handcuffed to the limitation on losses up to $25,000. That means if you have expenses of $100,000 for your rental property, and you are a passive real estate professional, your loss will be limited to $25,000. Yes, it hurts, but that is the tax law. However, if you are an active real estate professional, you can deduct the full $100,000! How do you qualify as an active professional?

The IRS has two tests for you to qualify as an active real estate professional:

Test 1: Are more than half of personal services in all businesses for the year performed in real property and rental real estate? This means if you have a job as a lawyer and own property, you will have to prove that you dedicate more than 51 percent of your time to the rental property.

Test 2: Does the taxpayer spend more than 750 hours in real property businesses and rentals in which he or she materially participates? In addition to the 51 percent test, you have to show that you spent more than 750 hours per year materially participating at the property. That means that you are the primary decision-maker or the person who goes to collect the rent, direct the contractor on repairs and improvements, handle all legal issues, and bear the responsibility to sign checks and approve expenses. This is even true if you hire a management company.

Conclusion

As you can see, there is a lot to learn. The Real Estate Professional Pocket Guide has only scratched the surface of the many scenarios you may encounter. But if you use all the valuable information in this guide, you will be on the road to real estate excellence.

APPENDIX

MACRS Recovery Period	
Type of Property	General Depreciation System
Computers and their peripheral equipment	5 years
Office machinery, such as typewriters, Calculators, Copiers	5 years
Automobiles	5 years
Light trucks	5 years
Appliances, such as Stoves, Refrigerators,	5 years
Carpets	5 years
Furniture used in rental property	5 years
Office furniture and equipment, such as Desks, Files	7 years

Any property that does not have a class life and that has not been designated bylaw as being in any other class	7 years
Roads	15 years
Shrubbery	15 years
Fences	15 years
Residential rental property (building or structure) and structural components, such as, furnaces, water pipes, venting, etc...	27.5 years

Additions and improvements, such as a new roof, have the same recovery period as that of the property to which the addition or improvement is made. This is determined as if the property was placed in service at the same time as the addition or improvement.

Record of Home Improvements

Keep this for your records. Also, keep receipts or other proof of improvements.

Example:

Home Improvements		
(a)	(b)	(c)

a. Type of Improvement

b. Date

c. Amount

The Next few pages will be dedicated to serving your home improvement needs and inspirations. Please utilize this part of the The Pocket Advisor as you see fit.

Home Improvements (For Your Use)		
(a)	(b)	(c)
Type of Improvement	Date	Amount
Additions		
Bedroom		
Bathroom		
Deck		
Garage		
Porch		
Patio		
Storage Shed		
Fireplace		
Other		
Lawn and Grounds		
Landscaping		
Driveway		
Walkway		
Fences		
Retaining Wall		
Sprinkler System		

Swimming Pool		
Exterior Lighting		
Other		
Communications		
Satellite Dish		
Intercom		
Security System		
Other		
Miscellaneous		
Storm Windows and Doors		
Central Vacuum		
Other		
Heating and Air Conditioning		
Heating System		
Central air Conditioning		
Furnace		
Ductwork		
Central Humidifier		
Filtration System		
Other		
Electrical		
Lighting Fixtures		

Wiring Upgrades		
Other		
Plumbing		
Water Heater		
Soft Water System		
Filtration System		
Other		
Insulation		
Attic		
Walls		
Floors		
Pipes and Ductwork		
Other		
Interior Improvements		
Built-in Appliances		
Kitchen Modernization		
Flooring		
Wall-to-wall Carpeting		
Bathroom Modernization		
Other		

INVESTOR TERMS TO KNOW

Know the Game

Building wealth is like building a house. You can do it brick by brick through your own labor, or you can have someone do some or all of it for you. When you have someone do it for you, or in this case, where there's an exchange for the use of your apartment, your tenant's monthly rent payments become the bricks to your financial house. This allows you to use your time focusing on other wealth-building activities or spend your free time enjoying the benefits of your activities.

When you have a rental property, the income you generate does not require your significant involvement. The ideal scenario is that you will receive rental income in excess of the expenses of operating your property and still have enough left over to invest or save. Of course, Uncle Sam will want his cut, too, which is where most people lose if they don't know the rules on keeping more of your money.

Here is a summary of terms you should know if you are thinking of incorporating rental properties into your wealth-building strategy. These are our explanations from an everyday perspective. We encourage you to use an on-line research platform of your choice to get their universal definitions.

Income: There are different types of income and they are all treated differently. Income can be earned actively from your own labor or from providing a product or service as part of your business. It can be earned as part of your investment portfolio or it can also be earned passively such as from royalties or renting the use of an asset such as an apartment. Passive income is income you make without working and this book will help you make it work for you!

Expenses: Costs incurred while generating income from an income-producing activity. The cost is typically in the form of a reduction of an asset such as cash. The reduction can be immediate or over time. If the use of the asset will extend beyond one year, then it is generally depreciated (see depreciation definition)

Asset: Tangible and intangible resources owned by an individual or business with future economic value and whose value can be measured in dollars at a particular point in time. In this book, the assets we generally refer to are cash, real estate, capital improvements, and appliances.

Liability: The amount owed to a lender or vendor in the future in exchange for an asset's purchase or use. Liabilities can be current or due within a time frame of less than one year, like when you buy supplies with your credit card. Liabilities can be in the form of long-term debt like a mortgage, which typically have fixed payment amounts and terms. Liabilities generally have an interest expense associated that you should keep track of and speak with your tax professional as to whether or not it can be deducted.

Equity: The difference between an asset(s) you own and what you owe on your asset(s). You gain equity by reducing any liabilities owed on the asset and/or increasing the asset's value through appreciation. If you take a mortgage out to purchase your investment property, your portion of the equity is the difference between what you purchased the property for and what you borrowed from the bank. Equity fluctuates depending on the position of liabilities securing the home as well as the current market. Equity is also called net worth.

Depreciation: For assets that have a useful life greater than one year, you generally have to allocate the cost over a predetermined number of years based on the asset class determined by the IRS

Deductible: For tax purposes, something is deductible when it is allowable as a deduction from taxable income by current tax law.

Audit: An IRS audit is an examination of your prior financial activities from a prior tax year to make sure these activities are consistent with the figures reported in your return for that year and in accordance with tax rules and law.

Balance Sheet: A statement of your net worth at a particular point in time calculated by taking the sum of all your assets less your liabilities at their current book values to determine your net equity position. If your liabilities exceed your assets, you are in a negative-equity position, which means you are in a deficit and may become insolvent, or worse, it could be game over. You want the individual and cumulative value of your assets to exceed your liabilities because then you will have enough resources to meet your current obligations and possibly enough in reserves for future obligations.

Check the balance sheet for the following:

» Ending Bank account balances for the rental property(s).

» Unpaid rent.

» Net book value of your rental property(s) after depreciation.

» Security deposits

» Mortgage balance(s)

Income Statement: If the balance sheet is analogous to a bank statement, then your income statement is the deposits (income) and withdrawals (expenses) section showing you from your last statement to your current statement what movements increased or decreased your balance. The goal is for your income to exceed your expenses for a net profit, which will flow through to your ending equity balance. However, because you are taxed on profits, the goal is to maximize your allowable deductions to reduce that final expense to Uncle Sam and keep more of your money.

Refer to the income statement for the following:

» All sources of income (Rent payments, Parking charged to tenants, interest from savings/investments)

» Your expenses for the year.

Books and Records: Record keeping is the foundation to be audit-proof. A famous lawyer said, "If the glove doesn't fit, you must acquit." To be acquitted means that you are legally blameless. In tax law, to be acquitted, you must have proof of income and expenses; or proof that you're keeping some kind of ongoing records. And in some unique cases, as a real estate investor, you have to have both.

• Tax law is law where the burden of proof is on you, not the IRS, which just has to propose you owe money, a polite way to say you owe money, and if you cannot prove it beyond a reasonable doubt, you will automatically owe it.

- Using the method of scanning your records and a bookkeeping tool or person is wise. And a significant step, in the following five steps:

  » Create a separate bank account for your rental income and expenses. This doesn't mean, create a separate entity for your rental property; separating your rental income and expenses shows an investor mindset.

  » Acquire an on-line bookkeeping tool or person to categorize the money that comes in and out of that separate bank account. Even if you live in the property, your accountant or tax software will ask your percentage of rental use, let them allocate it out for you. You're an investor, and your time is valuable.

  » Do your very best to keep proof of the money that comes in and out. You could have made a $500 purchase at a large hardware store near you on December 25th. The money could have come out of your separate bank account that day, and the IRS could not allow that expense. A receipt is the only document that can prove you did not purchase holiday supplies. There are unique situations where holiday supplies would be reasonable, ordinary, and necessary, but the point is you have the proof.

The life of your taxes: The IRS generally has three years from the due date of the tax return or from when the return was filed, if filed late, to audit a return. Taxpayers may claim a refund within three years from the date of the original deadline or two years from the date the tax was paid to claim a refund. Since Michael has owned his rental property for two years, he is within the time frame for either a refund or an audit.

The two key points to know is that:

- The IRS generally has three years from the date you filed your return to audit your return. This is even if you filed late. The key is to file on time to start the clock.

- To claim a refund from the IRS you only have three years from the due date of the tax return or two years from the payment of the tax. The key is that the IRS doesn't play fair, if you miss your due date the clock starts from that deadline date to claim your refund. You can be one day late to claim a refund of $100,000 and just not get it from the IRS.

About the Authors

Carlos Fraser, EA

Carlos F. Fraser, EA, is an Enrolled Agent with expertise in taxation for individuals, businesses, Non-for-profits, Estates & Trusts. His tax accounting career began at the ripe age of 16 years old--when he fell in love with the mixture of accounting and tax law and has never looked back. As a licensed Enrolled agent, like attorneys and Certified Public Accountants (CPAs), Carlos has unlimited rights to practice tax law. His responsibilities have a broad reach and afford him unrestricted authority to represent a breadth of taxpayers, tax matters and decide which IRS offices they can represent clients before.

Carlos' tenure includes leadership roles within a range of tax areas, Polo Ralph Lauren, as CFO of a not-for-profit church, and at CohnReznick LLP--one of the largest tax and advisory firms in the nation. Carlos has spent a significant portion of his career focused on IRS resolutions for complex, high net worth individuals and businesses.

Carlos is also a philanthropist who has dedicated his time to providing free tax services to low-income individuals through the IRS VITA program. His philanthropic efforts have also led him to provide free arbitration services to low-income individuals in U.S. Tax Court cases through the tax law firm Agostino & Associates Tax Clinic.

Now a partner of his own firm, Taxko, Inc., Carlos is committed to teaching and empowering his clients to build wealth and seize opportunities to pay the lowest tax amount under the law. He believes this can be achieved by generating growth, efficiency, and profitability for the business owner; by keeping them abreast of the constantly changing tax laws, legislation, and industry regulations. Carlos strongly feels that an informed client is a great client!

Cynthia Lubin,
CPA, MBA, Realtor Associate

Cynthia Lubin has over 15+ years of combined experience between Financial Services, Accounting, and Real Estate. Her passion for these areas came from lessons learned through her personal experience in overcoming financial challenges during her early adult years.

Throughout her graduate education and

professional experience, Cynthia bore witness to savvy individuals and companies who effectively applied financial principles that contributed to their success and financial stability. Early in her career, Cynthia's goal was to share her experience, knowledge, and expertise with the world!

Cynthia's finance journey began in 2004, where she worked as a loan officer for Starpoint Mortgage in Randolph, NJ. After the housing market collapsed in 2009, she transitioned to personal banking. As a personal banker, she began to learn more about managing personal finances to build wealth. Cynthia wanted to continue to expand her knowledge and decided to pursue her CPA. Her goal was to enhance her ability to better serve her clients in helping them build wealth.

Cynthia earned her MBA with a concentration in Professional Accounting from Rutgers University. She then went on to obtain her CPA. Cynthia spent time working for multiple Big Four Accounting firms and a Fortune100 Financial Services Company as an auditor and financial statement analyst.

After several years of working in Corporate America, Cynthia decided it was time to combine her real estate expertise with her financial knowledge and to kick-start her own business and service people within her community. She endeavored as an entrepreneur in May 2017, providing an eclectic mix of accounting and real estate services. Cynthia's goal is to create more financially savvy homeowners and educate people about managing their finances to build wealth.

CPSIA information can be obtained
at www.ICGtesting.com
Printed in the USA
LVHW022325030821
694243LV00007B/150